IMAGES
of America

MARYLAND IN THE CIVIL WAR

IMAGES
of America

MARYLAND IN
THE CIVIL WAR

Mark A. Swank and Dreama J. Swank

ARCADIA
PUBLISHING

Copyright © 2013 by Mark A. Swank and Dreama J. Swank
ISBN 978-1-4671-2041-8

Published by Arcadia Publishing
Charleston, South Carolina

Printed in the United States of America

Library of Congress Control Number: 2013935197

For all general information, please contact Arcadia Publishing:
Telephone 843-853-2070
Fax 843-853-0044
E-mail sales@arcadiapublishing.com
For customer service and orders:
Toll-Free 1-888-313-2665

Visit us on the Internet at www.arcadiapublishing.com

This book is dedicated to all of Maryland's sons and daughters that served on either side during the Civil War. Their service, along with the losses of everyday citizens and farmers who suffered greatly during the war, will forever be remembered in the photographs that will hopefully survive time's passing.

CONTENTS

ACKNOWLEDGMENTS

No book is complete without recognizing the numerous individuals that play a part in bringing the material together. First, we would like to thank all of the Civil War photojournalists that followed the armies through the war and took the photographs used in this book. Were it not for their efforts, the Civil War would not be remembered the way it is today. Mathew Brady, Alexander Gardner, Timothy O'Sullivan, James Gibson, and numerous other photojournalists are owed a debt of gratitude from all generations that followed.

We would like to thank the archivists at the US National Archives and the US Library of Congress for their excellent work in digitizing and making readily available many of the Civil War photographs used herein.

The aid of other organizations—like local historical societies; the Baltimore B&O Museum; and the US Army Heritage and Education Center, Carlisle Barracks, Pennsylvania—made it possible for us to find photographs that we would not have been able to include.

We would also like to thank our acquisitions editor, Lissie Cain, for keeping us on track with deadlines and helping us through the hurdles of putting the book together.

Lastly, we are indebted to our good friend Melissa "Missy" Thorseth for taking her personal time to review the content, provide new ideas, and make great recommendations for the book. Missy, a member of the Mason Dixon Line Preservation Partnership, organizes historical guided tours to local museums and mansions and participates in Civil War living history events. Her volunteer work includes crafting period letters to members of the 53rd Pennsylvania Volunteer Infantry and participating in the Memorial Illumination at Antietam National Battlefield, hosted every December. For her graduate degree project, she created an interactive website with links to all Maryland museums searchable by region or county.

All images in this volume appear courtesy of the US Library of Congress (LOC), the US National Archives and Records Administration (NARA), the US Army Heritage and Research Center (HRC), the Maryland State Archives (MSA), the Maryland Historical Society (MHS), or the Baltimore B&O Railroad Museum (B&O).

INTRODUCTION

With both US president Abraham Lincoln and Confederate president Jefferson Davis calling for soldiers to join the cause from their respective states, the Civil War would touch nearly every home in the North and the South. The war would last four long years and consume the entire Lincoln presidency. Over the course of the conflict, soldiers were initially mustered in for periods of three months and, later, for periods of up to one year. Many would volunteer over and over in support of their causes. In the end, the outcome of the war would be a rebirth of the nation, which would once again be the *United* States.

Maryland, along with the other border states of Delaware, Kentucky, and Missouri, would try to straddle the fence and not choose sides in the war. Times were prosperous, and Maryland generally desired to not get involved in the politics of differences between the southern states and the Federal government. But the events of April 19, 1861, would make that impossible as Baltimore would host the first combat casualty during the Civil War when attacks by Confederate sympathizers on Federal troops passing through the area would result in numerous deaths. This uprising would draw the line and force Lincoln to take drastic measures to ensure that Maryland supported the Federal government. In Baltimore, Confederate sympathizers were jailed and held indefinitely as Lincoln waived the writ of habeas corpus. Union occupation of Baltimore was swift and forceful. Federal units were positioned all over, and they dug themselves in. From the Susquehanna to Annapolis and then Relay, rail lines between Baltimore, Annapolis, and Washington were secured and heavily guarded with strong military presence and communication. Troops and supplies were reestablished, ending the opposition to the Union army between Washington and the North.

While Maryland saw its fair share of small skirmishes during the war, the Battle of Antietam would go down in history as its greatest battle. The loss of life at Antietam over the course of only 24 hours would be far greater than in any such period during any war before or after. Over the course of the next 150 years, a large part of the battlefields in and around Antietam would be converted from everyday farmland to a national park and memorial to those that fought and died during the battle.

Maryland would host numerous military encampments during the course of the war, with Baltimore alone having more than 40 installations. Point Lookout in St. Mary's County would be converted into a hospital and prisoner-of-war camp. The hospital would initially tend to Union soldiers wounded in battle, but later, as the prisoner-of-war camp was built, the hospital would also tend to the prisoners and guards at Point Lookout. Annapolis would host a major camp for paroled Union prisoners. The site, located near the intersection of routes 50 and 450, would receive and process soldiers brought from Confederate prisons near Richmond, Virginia. The parolees would arrive on flag-of-truce boats flying a white flag so they would not be considered military targets. Many of the arriving soldiers were wearing dirty, infested clothing and were emaciated from starvation and suffering from battle wounds. The first step upon arrival was to have them bathe in the river water and be provided new clothes. Next, they would receive a medical checkup at the College Green Barracks, located at St. John's College and occupied by the military. Those that needed immediate medical care would be sent to the army general hospital at the US Naval Academy. Those that did not need medical attention were then marched the two miles from the academy to the site of the parole camp.

Maryland railroads would also play an important role in the war effort. The Baltimore & Ohio (B&O) Railroad connected Washington, DC, with Baltimore and points north and supplied Washington with food and arms throughout the war. The Annapolis & Elk Ridge Railroad connected Annapolis with the B&O line at Annapolis Junction. Regimental guards were headquartered at Annapolis Junction, and the lines were protected by picket guards patrolling the railroad both day and night. The Relay House at Relay, Maryland, would also become a famous Civil War site. Union troops and artillery units were stationed there to protect the Thomas Viaduct across the Patapsco River from sabotage, and President Lincoln would change trains there on his way to visit Antietam Battlefield. John Surratt would pass through Relay when traveling to and from Canada.

Nearly all of the conspirators in the assassination of President Lincoln had roots in Maryland. Mary Surratt and her son John lived in Surrattsville for a time at the beginning of the war and later moved to Washington, DC, where Mary set up a boardinghouse. John used the move to Washington to gain better access to the capital for his espionage activities. Samuel Mudd was born in Charles County, Maryland, and attended a boarding school in Frederick, Maryland. He studied medicine at the University of Maryland in Baltimore, and after the assassination of Lincoln, he would set, splint, and bandage Lincoln's assassin's broken leg. John Wilkes Booth, Lincoln's assassin, was born near Bel Air, Maryland. He attended a boarding school for boys in Sparks, Maryland, and later a military academy school in Catonsville, Maryland. He is buried in the family plot at Green Mount Cemetery in Baltimore.

One

MARYLAND AS
A BORDER STATE

At the outset of the war, Maryland was undecided on its allegiance to either side in the dispute over slavery. Counties in the north and west tended to be antislavery, while counties in the south and on the Eastern Shore tended to be proslavery. Even though Maryland was a slave state, it chose to not secede from the Union. However, Maryland loyalties were so divided at the start of the war that the state supplied over 60,000 soldiers to the Union military and more than 25,000 to the Confederate military.

After the Baltimore Riot of April 19, 1861, President Lincoln recognized the importance of Maryland remaining a part of the Union and sent troops to Baltimore to quell the riots and institute martial law over the city. In September 1861, more than one third of the Maryland General Assembly was arrested, along with other Baltimore officials, for being secessionists. Had Lincoln not taken the action to institute martial law and arrest the secessionists, Maryland may have seceded from the Union, resulting in Washington, DC, being completely surrounded by Confederate states and cut off from the other Union states. This would almost certainly have resulted in the Union capital moving out of Washington, DC, if not the complete dissolution of the Union. It was not until 1864 that Maryland would adopt a new state constitution outlawing the practice of slavery and extending the right to vote to nonwhite males.

On April 18, 1861, Pennsylvania volunteer soldiers were hooted and pelted with stones and bricks as they marched from President Street Station to Camden Street Station. The next day, two more regiments arrived, answering their call from President Lincoln to protect the capital. Four companies of the 6th Massachusetts Volunteer Militia were set upon by a mob on Pratt Street and opened fire, killing a dozen civilians before police were able to subdue the rioters long enough for the troops to board their trains at Camden Station and continue their movement to the capital. At the end of the day, 4 soldiers from the 6th Massachusetts and 12 Baltimore residents were killed during the riot, making Baltimore the site of the first bloodshed of the American Civil War. (Both, LOC.)

A former slave, Nicholas Biddle was an orderly to the company commander of the Washington Artillerists of Pottsville, Pennsylvania. He was severely injured during the Baltimore attacks of April 18, 1861. When the Pennsylvanian volunteers arrived in Washington, DC, the next morning, President Lincoln personally came to the Capitol to thank them. When he saw Nicholas's injuries, he took his hand and recommended he receive immediate medical attention. (LOC.)

THE REBEL CHIVALRY

The effects of the war and the opinions of those in the North were far different than those in the South. In Maryland, the uniforms of soldiers of the North were viewed far differently by pro-Union media than those of their Southern counterparts. In this 1862 print published in *Harper's Weekly*, a finely dressed US soldier and his majestic horse stand in comparison to the tattered uniform of a Confederate soldier and his malnourished steed. (LOC.)

George P. Kane was the chief of police for Baltimore during the Baltimore Riot of 1861. He was later arrested for suspicion of treason, along with the mayor and entire city council of Baltimore, on June 27, 1861, and detained at Fort McHenry. Kane was eventually released in 1862 and would later run for and be appointed mayor of Baltimore in 1877. (MSA.)

Thomas H. Hicks was governor of Maryland from 1858 to 1862. After the Baltimore Riot, it was suggested to Governor Hicks by the mayor of Baltimore and the police marshal that the railroad bridges leading into the city be burned to stop the flow of Union troops. Hicks ordered 1st Lt. John Merryman of the Baltimore County Horse Guards to burn the bridges. (NARA.)

On the afternoon of April 19, 1861, after the Baltimore Riot, Governor Hicks and Baltimore mayor George W. Brown sent this telegram to President Lincoln, notifying him of the chaotic events of that day. They specifically asked that no more Union troops be allowed to pass through Maryland and note that they have called out the state troops in Baltimore to preserve the peace. The following day, President Lincoln replied that Gen. Winfield Scott would "march them around Baltimore, and not through it." Hick's loyalties were clearly divided at this point; the telegram states that they are trying to preserve the peace, but at the same time he was ordering the burning of the bridges leading into Baltimore. (LOC.)

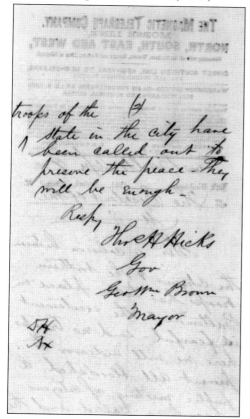

Gen. Benjamin Butler was dispatched along with a Massachusetts Infantry Regiment to secure communication and transportation lines around Baltimore. On the April 20, 1861, they arrived at Annapolis, Maryland. By April 22, 1861, Butler had negotiated with Governor Hicks for the repair of the railroads already destroyed. Units of the 8th New York Regiment, now under control of General Butler, then entrenched themselves around the Thomas Viaduct near Relay, Maryland, to secure the railroad lines between the capital and Baltimore. On May 14, without orders, Butler had troops occupy Baltimore and control the Federal Hill area by placing camps on high ground to support the artillery at Fort McHenry. Before long, Baltimore was placed under martial law to quell the secessionists. Gen. Winfield Scott would relieved Butler of his command over the occupation of Baltimore. However, President Lincoln promoted Butler several days later and assigned him to duty in Virginia. Later in the war, Butler would declare runaway slaves from Virginia as "contraband" and refuse to return them to their owners. (LOC.)

During the war, numerous forts and camps were set up in defense of Baltimore. Fort Marshall, shown in this lithograph print from 1861, was erected as an eastern defense of Baltimore on Murray Hill, also known as Snake Hill or Potter's Hill, located in present-day Highlandtown, opposite Fort McHenry. The fort was built in the shape of a four-pointed star. The 7th Maine Regiment, pictured in this scene, camped here during September and October 1861. The fort's 38 heavy guns guarded the city from attack from Baltimore Harbor. Fort Marshall's guns, along with those at Fort McHenry and Federal Hill, were also used as a deterrent against rebellion from within the city. The fort was later occupied by the 5th New York Volunteer Artillery in 1862 and abandoned in late 1864 just prior to the end of the war. Today, the land once occupied by Fort Marshall is home to the Sacred Heart of Jesus Roman Catholic Church. (LOC.)

After occupying the Annapolis & Elkridge Railroad depot at Annapolis, General Butler began the work of repairing the damages committed by Maryland's secessionists. Locomotive engines were repaired at the depot while two companies of the 8th Massachusetts pushed a handcar loaded with tools down the tracks toward Annapolis Junction. All along the way they repaired tracks and bridges destroyed by the secessionists. In this print from *Frank Leslie's Illustrated Newspaper*, Frank Pierce, a soldier from the 8th Massachusetts Regiment, is shown diving in a creek looking for a missing rail as soldiers repair the bridge and rails. Along the way they came across a bridge at Millersville that had been destroyed. After taking nearly a full day to repair the bridge, the soldiers of the 8th Massachusetts, along with soldiers of the 7th New York, arrived at Annapolis Junction on April 25, 1861, having taken only two days to repair the damaged Annapolis & Elkridge Railroad lines. (LOC.)

The Baltimore & Ohio Railroad connected Washington, DC, with Baltimore and points north and was the main transportation route for providing Washington with food, supplies, and soldiers. In a strategic move to protect the movement of Federal troops into Washington, DC, Annapolis Junction, Maryland, was occupied on April 25, 1861, by soldiers from the 7th New York and the 8th Massachusetts. These soldiers, commanded by General Butler, had left Annapolis the day before after taking possession of the Annapolis & Elkridge Railway. They marched the 21-mile stretch through the night, repairing the tracks and bridges where needed, and arrived at Annapolis Junction the following day. Guard duty along the railroad lines was monotonous and boring work but was a key factor in stopping secessionists from destroying the railroads. This print, published in *Frank Leslie's Illustrated Newspaper*, depicts the troop's camp and occupation of Annapolis Junction. (LOC.)

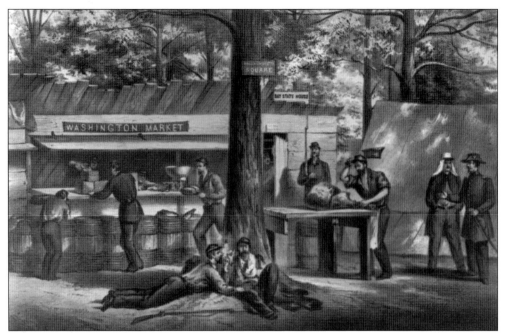

The Union, recognizing the importance of the B&O Railroad as a major supply line to the capital, garrisoned troops from Massachusetts and New York at Relay, Maryland, to secure and guard this vital area. This print depicts the commissary set up near the Relay House to support the Union troops. (LOC.)

This practice battery of guns at the US Naval Academy was used to train cadets when they were not at sea. Fearing an attack on the academy by Southern sympathizers, superintendent Capt. George S. Blake had the gun battery removed, along with all arms, ammunition, and ordnance stores, to the USS *Constitution*. (NARA.)

The Tripoli Monument, pictured here in 1860, continues to stand on the grounds of the US Naval Academy in Annapolis. Originally erected in 1808 at the Washington Navy Yard, the monument was commissioned as a memorial to the six naval officers who died fighting the Barbary pirates during the First Barbary War (1801–1805). In 1831, the monument was moved to its permanent home at the US Naval Academy, where it sits today between Leahy Hall and Preble Hall. (NARA.)

The USS *Santee* (left) and USS *Constitution* are pictured at the US Naval Academy in Annapolis, Maryland, at the start of the Civil War. The USS *Constitution* was used as a training vessel for midshipmen at the academy. For security reasons, the US Naval Academy would be moved to Fort Adams in Newport, Rhode Island, in late April 1861 and stay there for the remainder of the war. (NARA.)

On May 13, 1861, Gen. Benjamin Butler had members of the 6th Massachusetts Regiment occupy Baltimore under martial law to take control of the city and eliminate any further riots by its citizens. By the next day, the Federal Hill area of Baltimore was swarming with camps and Union troops. This picture shows the troops of the 6th Massachusetts Regiment camped around Monument Square. The next day, Butler would send this message to the commander at Fort McHenry: "I have taken possession of Baltimore. My troops are on Federal Hill, which I can hold with the aid of my artillery. If I am attacked tonight, please open upon Monument Square with your mortars." A large contingent of military camps would remain in Baltimore for the remainder of the war. (LOC.)

The print depicts the arrest of Baltimore's marshal of police, George Kane, for suspicion of treason. Kane was taken from his home on St. Paul Street at 3:00 a.m. on June 27, 1861, by members of the Pennsylvania and Massachusetts Regiments and was initially incarcerated at Fort McHenry. After his arrest, General Banks issued a proclamation to the people of Baltimore superseding Kane's official authority as chief of police and appointed Colonel Kenly as his replacement "for the time being." Kane would later be moved to Fort Lafayette in New York. While imprisoned in New York, he would write to Abraham Lincoln, complaining about the conditions: "Whilst suffering great agony from the promptings of nature and effects of my debility I am frequently kept for a long time at the door of my cell waiting for permission to go to the water-closet owing to the utter indifference of some of my keepers to the ordinary demands of humanity." He was then moved again to Fort Warren in Boston, Massachusetts, until being released in 1862. (LOC.)

Fort McHenry served as a military prison during the Civil War. Political figures and citizens of Baltimore who were suspected of having secessionist views were arrested and confined there without charge. One of those detainees, John Merryman, was ordered by the governor of Maryland to burn the railroad bridges north of Baltimore to stop the flow of Federal soldiers through the city. Major Moore, commander of Fort McHenry at the start of the war, suspended the writ of habeas corpus for the detainees, a move that would be challenged by Supreme Court chief justice Roger B. Taney. During the war, Fort McHenry was also used as an artillery training area. Gen. Benjamin Butler would call upon the commander of Fort McHenry to shell Federal Hill in Baltimore should Butler's units come under attack by the citizens of the city. (LOC.)

Two

WARTIME INTELLIGENCE

Throughout the war, numerous mechanisms were employed by both sides to gain intelligence and subvert the enemy. Having been trained by Federal organizations prior to secession, Southern intelligence organizations were able to direct their resources appropriately and target Federal weaknesses. One such example was the use of signal officers on the battlefield. Through the use of the signal towers and the wigwag signaling system, commanders on the field were able to communicate with other commanders nearby and direct the battle. Southern signal officers were able to read northern flag movements and counter their attacks.

The Secret Service came into being at the turn of the Civil War. Allen Pinkerton formed the organization and provided valuable intelligence—both from the field and back in Washington—to Abraham Lincoln. In Washington, Pinkerton and his men were constantly on the lookout for spies among the masses. Those that were captured in the act or suspected of espionage were usually arrested and sent to a prison set up at the former Arsenal Building in Washington. It was at this prison that four Lincoln conspirators would eventually be hanged.

John Surratt was engaged in Confederate intelligence activities at the start of the war. Initially, he would provide information on troop movements in southern Maryland near his family home in Surrattsville, where he lived with his mother, Mary, and his sister Anna. Later, when Mary Surratt packed up the family and moved to Washington, DC, John's role in Confederate intelligence changed to include being a courier of secret messages from Confederate headquarters in Richmond, Virginia, to a Confederate base of operations in Canada where Gen. Edwin G. Lee was stationed. John would make numerous train trips from Washington to Canada over the course of the war.

One famous Civil War intelligence activity that has become overlooked with the passing of time is the planned kidnapping of Abraham Lincoln by John Wilkes Booth and his coconspirators. Booth laid out plans for the kidnapping and even went so far as to implement it. It failed, however, because Lincoln was to have been captured on his way back from a play at Campbell Military Hospital outside of Washington but changed his plans and attended a ceremony at the National Hotel instead. Many historians believe that it was this failed kidnapping that led Booth to change his plans to an assassination of Abraham Lincoln.

These unidentified scouts and guides of the Army of the Potomac worked under the direction of Allan Pinkerton of the US Secret Service. They would make their way quietly into the Confederate camps under disguise to gather information about Rebel forces and then make their way back to Union forces with the important information. (NARA.)

This photograph, taken in October 1862, shows Union Signal Corps men Lt. Edward C. Pierce (left) and Lieutenant Rockwell (center) sitting with John C. Babcock (right) of the US Secret Service Department at Elk Mountain, Maryland. The Signal Corps and Secret Service men worked closely throughout the war. Babcock was actually a civilian but was often called by the title of "Lieutenant" or "Captain." (LOC.)

Rosie O'Neal Greenhow, pictured here with her daughter "Little Rose" at the Old Capital Prison in Washington, DC, was a spy for the Confederate States of America. Originally born in Port Tobacco, Maryland, during the war she lived in Washington, DC, where she was recruited and provided a 26-symbol cipher for encoding her secret messages. She was arrested by Allan Pinkerton on August 23, 1861. She and her daughter were released and deported to Richmond, Virginia, on May 31, 1862. She later toured Britain and France to generate support for the Confederate cause. While in London, she had her memoirs published; they were well received and brought her a good fortune. In 1864, after traveling Europe, she boarded the British blockade runner *Condor* and headed back to the United States. When the boat ran aground near Wilmington, North Carolina, Greenhow fled in a rowboat, which capsized. She drowned and was later buried with full military honors in the Oakdale Cemetery in Wilmington, North Carolina. (LOC.)

Shortly after the Battle of Antietam, President Lincoln visited the battlefield. In this photograph, he is shown posing with Gen. John A. McClernand (right) and Allan Pinkerton (left) outside of McClernand's tent. Before the war, McClernand had been a politician from Illinois and a close friend of President Lincoln. In 1864, he would leave the army and serve as a judge and politician. Allan Pinkerton was head of the Union Intelligence Service and often used the pseudonym "Maj. E.J. Allen" when working undercover himself. The intelligence service was the forerunner of today's US Secret Service. Prior to the war, Pinkerton was responsible for Lincoln's bypassing Baltimore when traveling from Illinois for the 1860 inauguration as he had discovered a plot to assassinate Lincoln during the transit through the city. Pinkerton is a member of the Military Intelligence Hall of Fame. (LOC.)

Allan Pinkerton (first row, far left) is pictured with unidentified visitors from Washington, DC, at the battlefield at Antietam. They had probably come to discuss the battle as well as other events in Washington, DC. When not with the Army of the Potomac in the field, Pinkerton spent most of his time in the capital tracking down Confederate spies and Rebel sympathizers. (LOC.)

This photograph, taken in October 1862, shows Secret Service man John C. Babcock and his celebrated warhorse Gimlet. In February 1863, Babcock would be instrumental in working with Col. George H. Sharpe, deputy provost marshal for the Army of the Potomac, in the creation of the new Bureau of Military Intelligence for the Union. (LOC.)

At Antietam, Maryland, operatives of the US Secret Service posed for this photograph in October 1862. The Secret Service played an active role during the Civil War in gathering intelligence about the enemy, sometimes disguising themselves as the enemy and walking right into the Rebel camps as they gathered vital intelligence. Pictured in front of the tent are, from left to right, (seated) R. William Moore and Allan Pinkerton; (standing) George H. Bangs, John C. Babcock, and Augustus K. Littlefield. Bangs was general superintendent of Pinkerton's team of operatives. Prior to the breakout of war, Pinkerton himself was responsible for identifying the plot to assassinate Abraham Lincoln at Baltimore while the president elect was on his way to Washington, DC, for his inauguration. (LOC.)

During the Battle of Antietam, the Union's Signal Corps set up a signal tower on top of Elk Mountain. The makeshift tower was built out of local tree stock and provided an excellent view of the battle as it unfolded. In the foreground, note the stumps of the trees used to build the tower. This photograph was taken a few days after the battle had occurred in September 1862. Lt. Edward C. Pierce is seen using his collapsible telescope to monitor the battlefield area for possible skirmishes. Alexander Gardner would later use this photograph in his famous *Photographic Sketch Book of the War*, in which he would write, "The Elk Mountain Signal Station was operated by Lieutenants Pierce and Jerome, and the view was taken whilst the former officer was receiving a dispatch from General McClellan, probably requesting further information in regard to some reported movement of his wary foe, or sending an important order to a Corps Commander." (LOC.)

This photograph, also taken at the Elk Mountain Signal Tower a few days after the battle, shows the signal station receiving a dispatch from another station. Flag holders would use specific flag movements called wigwag signaling to spell out messages relayed from the signal officer. These messages, sometimes referred to as dispatches, were then passed between headquarters and the commanders on the battlefield. The telescope used by Lieutenant Pierce in the photograph on the preceding page can be seen in this photograph as well, sitting idle on top of the tower. One Rebel correspondent later wrote about the Antietam signal towers, "Their signal stations on the Blue Ridge commanded a view of our every movement. We could not make a maneuver in front or rear against the moving columns. It was this information, conveyed by the little flags upon the mountain-top, that no doubt enabled the enemy to concentrate his force against our weakest points, and counteract the effect of whatever similar movements may have been attempted by us." (LOC.)

During the war, signal officers would use all means available to acquire information about enemy troop movements. Sometimes, the most advantageous lookout point would be on the roof of a house. This print depicts one example of a Union signal officer in the attic of a farmhouse, watching Confederate general Robert E. Lee's army near Williamsport, Maryland. (LOC.)

Officers of the Union Secret Service Department are pictured at their camp headquarters at Antietam in October 1862. Identified in the picture are Allan Pinkerton, head of the Secret Service Department (standing to the left of the tent pole), and John C. Babcock (second from left). (LOC.)

This photograph, taken near the Point of Rocks, Maryland, provided a great view of the Pleasant Valley area. Two Union signal officers monitored the surrounding area for Confederate movement. It is believed that this station was the first to detect Confederate J.E.B. Stuart's cavalry crossing the Potomac back into Virginia on October 12, 1862, after their raids into Maryland and Pennsylvania. In addition to providing early warnings of advancing enemy, the signal officers played an active role in the receipt and transmission of battlefield dispatches. The signal officers would set up multiple signal stations on high ground that would afford them an unobstructed view of the battlefield and opposing forces. When needed, local trees were cut down and the timber was used to quickly construct towers upon which the flagman and signal officers would perch to observe the battle as it progressed. (LOC.)

While many people recognized John Surratt as playing some part in the assassination of President Lincoln, what most do not know is that he was actually a Confederate Secret Service courier and spy. After the war, he admitted to carrying documents from the headquarters of the Confederacy in Richmond, Virginia, to Confederates in Canada. He was also involved in spy activities at the Federal prisoner-of-war camp at Elmira, New York. Surratt was asked by Confederate general Edwin G. Lee to go to Elmira and gather intelligence about the prisoner-of-war camp there. Plans were in the works to launch a daring attack on the prison to release the much-needed Confederate soldiers being held. The raid never took place, but Surratt managed to sketch detailed drawings of the camp and provide the critical intelligence that Lee needed. (NARA.)

Elmira Prison in New York played an important role in the life of Maryland Confederate spy John Surratt. After the war, Surratt gave a lecture at a Rockville, Maryland, courthouse, detailing his involvement in the scheme to kidnap Lincoln and his spy work for Gen. Edwin G. Lee but continuing to deny any knowledge of the assassination plot with John Wilkes Booth. He claimed that General Lee, while in Canada, tasked him with sketching the Elmira Prison and determining the number of prisoners, the number of guards that were on duty, and the type of arms that were used to protect the facility. All of this was so that an attempt could be made to free the prisoners that were so desperately needed by the Confederacy to continue the war. (LOC.)

Three

BATTLES AND SKIRMISHES

Maryland endured its fair share of battles and skirmishes over the course of the war. Conservative estimates put the number of engagements at somewhere around 75. Many of the raids into Maryland were by Confederate forces attempting to disrupt communications and supply lines into Washington, DC. Bridges, railroads, and telegraph lines were easy targets for the Confederate raiders. In most cases, the disruption was only temporary as the North became efficient at repairing the damages.

While most of the activity in Maryland during the war was in the form of small raids and skirmishes, by far the largest, most photographed, and most remembered event is the Battle of Antietam. More Americans died in that battle than would in any other one-day period in US military history. Alexander Gardner traveled to Antietam to see and photograph the devastation, and the photographs he took would be a grim reminder for all generations to come. Two weeks after the battle ended, Pres. Abraham Lincoln also visited the battlefield, traveling from Washington, DC, to the Relay House, where he changed trains and continued on to Antietam. The president spent four days at Antietam, discussing the events with his military commanders, witnessing the destruction to the surrounding communities, and visiting the wounded.

After the battle, Gardner walked amongst the fields and camps to get his poignant photographs. These images tell a story of historic battle, horrific deaths, the destruction wrought upon local farm fields and buildings, and even camp life for officers and soldiers who posed for the camera.

In late 1862, Confederate general Stonewall Jackson was looking for an easy target to disrupt the Federal supply of coal to Washington, DC. Late on the night of December 7, 1862, the 27th Virginia Militia attempted to destroy Dam No. 5 of the C&O Canal, near Williamsport, Maryland. This print, sketched by an artist and member of the 13th Massachusetts, depicts the events of that attempt. (LOC.)

After the Battle of Gettysburg, Confederate general Robert E. Lee's army was in retreat back to Virginia. Over the next week, several skirmishes would take place as Union general George G. Meade's army was advancing on Williamsport. This print depicts the July 6, 1863, charge of the 6th Michigan Cavalry over the Confederate breastworks near Falling Waters on the Maryland side of the Potomac. (LOC.)

In late June 1862, the 22nd New York State Militia was ordered to Maryland Heights, across the river from Harper's Ferry. The unit had previously been stationed at Camp Monroe, Patterson Park, Baltimore, with the task of aiding in the securing of the city. These images show the unit at Maryland Heights performing daily drills. Blank cartridges were used for drills so as to give the horses of the cavalry the experience of the noise and smoke of battle. During the morning, the unit would perform company drills for three hours. In the afternoon, they would perform battalion and brigade drills. All together, they would practice drill six days a week for a total of six hours a day. (Both, HRC.)

In this photograph taken after the Battle of Antietam was over, two Confederate soldiers lie where they died defending a bridge. At what would later be called Burnside's Bridge, fewer than 350 soldiers of the 2nd Georgia Infantry Regiment and the 20th Georgia Infantry Regiment held off Union general Ambrose Burnside's advancing IX Corps for more than four hours on the morning of September 17, 1862. (LOC.)

Confederate dead on Miller's Farm after the Battle of Antietam are lined up and awaiting burial. It was not unusual for Confederate dead to be buried by Union soldiers in mass graves near where they died. Most were buried with little identification on their grave markers. Nearly all Union dead would later be reinterred in the Antietam National Cemetery, while Confederate dead would later be reinterred at other local cemeteries. (LOC.)

Confederate soldiers from Brig. Gen. William E. Starke's Louisiana Brigade lie dead along the west side of Hagerstown Turnpike, some 500 yards north of the Dunker Church, Antietam, Maryland. Starke's brigade initially held off Federal advances by Brig. Gen. John Gibbon's 4th Brigade but was later forced to withdraw under heavy return fire from Gibbon's "Iron Brigade." After the wounding of Gen. John R. Jones, Starke would take command of the division and personally lead the men up the road to counterattack the enemy. In a hail of Federal fire, Starke would be knocked off his horse and wounded three times. He would die within the hour. The Hagerstown Pike can be seen in the photograph above on the side of the rail fence opposite the soldiers. In the same photograph, the dirt road to the left of the soldiers is a farm road on Miller's Farm. (Both, LOC.)

Confederate dead, probably from General Starke's Louisiana Brigade, at Antietam lie along the Hagerstown Pike fence. These men are part of the same group from the upper photograph on the preceding page. Famed photographer Alexander Gardner is credited with taking nearly all of the Antietam Battlefield photographs in circulation today. A Union soldier later wrote home that the dead were moved off the road and along the fence so that the road could be made passable. (LOC.)

This Confederate soldier was wounded in the Battle of Antietam and managed to drag himself to a small hillside ravine before dying. This solemn image of the contorted body of a single dead soldier provides a drastic contrast to the other photographs taken by Alexander Gardner of multiple dead at Antietam. (LOC.)

Known as the "Sunken Road" by local farmers before the war and "Bloody Lane" after the war, this Antietam Battlefield farm road near Roulette's Farm was filled with Confederate dead prior to burial. One Union soldier later remarked that there were so many bodies that one could walk across them for as far as the eye could see without touching the ground. In the photograph below, the soldiers standing along the ditch were probably members of the 145th Pennsylvania, which was assigned burial detail on the day these pictures were taken. It took a full week to bury all of the dead from the battle, and many burials were hastily done, with some in long trenches like those shows here. Roulette's Farm alone was said to have more than 700 dead buried in its fields. (Both, LOC.)

Prior to the Battle at Antietam, famed special artist Alfred R. Waud captured on print as Union Scouts monitored the Army of Northern Virginia crossing the Potomac near White's Ford. Waud would later describe the arriving Confederates "as a body handsome, athletic men, but generally polite and agreeable in manner". (LOC.)

A single Union soldier's grave is seen near the foot of a tree. The soldiers standing appear to be overlooking the vast battlefield and carnage of the fierce fighting that took place the day before. Two other soldiers lie on the ground resting; they are probably part of the burial detail that dug the grave. (LOC.)

This Antietam Battlefield photograph shows the spot where General Sumner's corps charged across the open field in an attempt to take the West Woods. The Confederates would counter the attack and repel Sumner's advances. The picket fence lies in ruin along with the dead horses and men. A broken Rebel artillery gun carriage sits idle after the battle. The Antietam Battlefield Park Visitor Center sits today where this photograph was taken. (LOC.)

While photographing the battlefield at Antietam, Alexander Gardner took a photograph of a single dead horse that at first glance appeared to be simply resting. Gardner would caption the image simply, "Dead Horse of Confederate Colonel, both killed at Battle of Antietam." Historians now believe the horse belonged to Confederate colonel Henry B. Strong of the 6th Louisiana Infantry. (LOC.)

A Union soldier stands near a row of graves of fellow Union soldiers that lost their lives trying to cross the Lower Bridge at Antietam. Georgia Infantry Regiments held off Gen. Ambrose Burnside's advancing 9th Corps at this bridge on the morning of September 17, 1862. The bridge was eventually taken after three hours as Burnside's men rushed the narrow structure. Confederate reinforcements arrived just in time to delay the 9th Corps, which was busy attacking the Georgians on the right flank. Nearly 500 Union soldiers were either killed or wounded in taking the crossing. The bridge, later known as Burnside's Bridge, is visible in the background, behind the standing soldier. The graves in the photograph were identified with simple wood markers. Burnside Bridge continued to be used until the mid-1960s, when it was closed to vehicular traffic to preserve its structure and historical value. (LOC.)

In the photograph above, an Antietam burial detail looks upon the dead as one soldier digs a grave. A single grave can be seen to the left of the standing soldiers. With pickaxes and shovels, the task of burying those that had died would last for days. Note the soldiers' rifles on the right, leaning against each other to keep the barrels off the ground. In the photograph below, another burial detail looks upon the battle debris and dead near a small tree mound. One soldier on burial detail would later write that the sight and smell of the bloated bodies was sickening. (Both, LOC.)

A Union soldier stands over the grave of a fellow Federal soldier who died near this tree. In contrast, a Confederate soldier lies unburied nearby. Union soldiers were the first to be interred. The task of identifying the dead was as hastily done as the burial itself and was accomplished by referencing uniforms and unit insignia along with letters or photographs that the dead had on them. (LOC.)

Confederate artillery soldiers killed at Antietam lie near a damaged wagon and the dead horse that was pulling it. The Dunker Church, seen in the background, was the site of fierce fighting during the battle, a field hospital for Confederate wounded, and later a truce location for the exchange of dead and injured. After the war, soldiers returning to Antietam for reunions would remember the day's battles and pose in front of the church for photographs. (LOC.)

This battlefield photograph was taken near the Sherrick House at Antietam near Burnside Bridge. After General Burnside took the lower bridge, he marched his corps across the Sherricks' farm toward Sharpsburg to cut off Confederate general Robert E. Lee's retreating forces. The 79th New York Volunteers fought near the house after crossing Antietam Creek and suffered only 40 casualties, a small number considering the heaving losses at Antietam. (LOC.)

An idle artillery unit in formation waits in an open field the day after the Battle of Antietam. A man with binoculars, probably a scout or signal officer, sits on a hilltop near McClellan's headquarters, looking toward Antietam Creek. The idle artillery unit is probably part of Union general Andrew A. Humphreys' 5th Corps division. Campfires can be seen in the background. (LOC.)

Capt. Joseph M. Knap's Pennsylvania Light Artillery, Independent Battery E is seen in this photograph at Antietam after the battle. During heavy fighting, one section of Knap's battery was temporarily detached to come to the aid of Union general George S. Greene. Greene's men fought Stonewall Jackson's soldiers near Dunker Church and made advances against Jackson's line further than any other Union unit. (LOC.)

Col. Turner G. Morehead of the 106th Pennsylvania Volunteers is pictured at Antietam on September 19, 1862, two days after the battle. Morehead was born at Baltimore, Maryland, on March 18, 1814, and later moved to Philadelphia, Pennsylvania. At the start of the war, he commanded a regiment of the 22nd Pennsylvania Volunteers, which performed duties as provost guards when Baltimore was occupied by federal soldiers shortly after the riots of April 19, 1861. (LOC.)

Two weeks after the Battle of Antietam, President Lincoln visited the battlefield and spent several days talking to the generals and soldiers that fought in the fields and surrounding area of Sharpsburg, Maryland. In this photograph taken by Alexander Gardner, the president is seen talking with Gen. George B. McClellan in the general's tent. A US flag is seen on a table, while a captured Rebel flag can be seen on the ground in front of it. Lincoln criticized McClellan for not destroying Lee's army at Antietam and would eventually relieve him of command as general in chief and commander of the Army of the Potomac. McClellan would be nominated for president on the Democratic ticket in 1864 and would run unsuccessfully against Lincoln. His battlefield capabilities would be called into question for years to come, and Ulysses S. Grant would later say of him, "McClellan is to me one of the mysteries of the war." (LOC.)

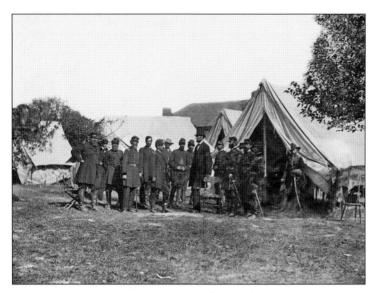

During his visit to the Antietam Battlefield, President Lincoln posed with General McClellan and other officers of the Army of the Potomac. The man standing on the far right is Capt. George Armstrong Custer. At six feet four inches, Abraham Lincoln was the tallest US president. His height is quite evident in this photograph, where he seems to tower over the officers. (LOC.)

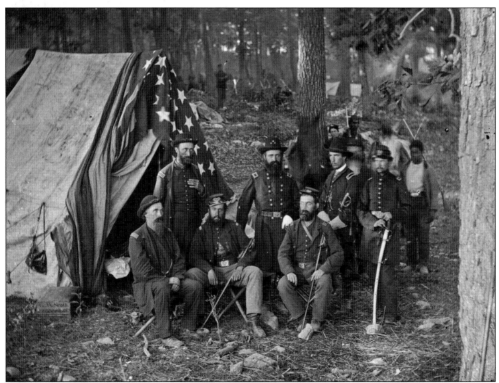

Union general John C. Caldwell (fourth from left) and his staff are pictured at their Antietam camp after the battle. General Caldwell was only 28 years old when, having no prior military background, he joined the military in 1861. He would command a brigade at Antietam and be wounded during battle; he would later be criticized for his assault on Bloody Lane. (LOC.)

Union general Randolf B. Marcy is seen here with officers and civilians at the headquarters of the Army of the Potomac at Antietam Battlefield. Pictured are, from left to right, Capt. Wright Rives, John W. Garrett (president of the Baltimore & Ohio Railroad), an unidentified orderly, General Marcy, Lt. Col. Andrew P. Porter, Col. Thomas S. Mather, Ozias M. Hatch, and Joseph C.G. Kennedy. (LOC.)

The 93rd New York Infantry pose for a unit photograph after drill practice at the headquarters of the Army of the Potomac at Antietam following the battle. One soldier later wrote home about their drill commander, "The Major is a splendidly drilled officer having been in the service at least thirty years, and it is a great privilege to get the benefit of his knowledge." (LOC.)

Members of the 93rd New York Volunteers pose for a photograph outside of their tent at Antietam Battlefield. It appears that Col. John S. Crocker (seated, left) is being offered a cigar by Lt. Col. Benjamin C. Butler while Butler's adjutant watches. Crocker was captured by Confederate forces in early 1862 and spent four months at Libby Prison in Richmond, Virginia, before being paroled. (LOC.)

Lt. Col. Charles B. Norton sits on his horse at the headquarters of Gen. Fitz John Porter at Antietam. Norton was assigned to the 5th Corps of the Army of the Potomac under the direction of General Porter on August 20, 1862. The 5th Corps fought at Second Battle at Bull Run in late August 1862 and in a reserve position for McClellan's Army of the Potomac during the Maryland Campaign at Antietam. Porter resigned from the army on January 6, 1863. (LOC.)

A blacksmith at the headquarters of the Army of the Potomac at Antietam can be seen shoeing horses. At the start of the war, 104 out of the 176 cavalry officers resigned to join the Confederacy, leaving the Union forces at a major disadvantage in equestrian experience. Depots such as Geisboro Point Cavalry Depot (site of the US Defense Intelligence Agency today) were established to supply horses to the Union army. (LOC.)

Posing in front of a tent at Antietam Battlefield are, from left to right, (first row) Union officers Lt. Rufus King, Lt. Alonzo Cushing, and Lt. Evan Thomas; (second row) three other artillery officers. Lieutenants King and Cushing would later be awarded the Medal of Honor for their actions during the war. (LOC.)

This print, also by Alfred R. Waud, depicts an Army of the Potomac encampment at Harpers Ferry as seen at night, with a view of Maryland Heights in the background. The Battle of Harpers Ferry was fought September 12–15, 1862, as part of the Maryland Campaign and was a precursor to the fierce fighting that would happen at Antietam less than a week later. Waud would later be recognized as one of only two artists present during the Battle of Gettysburg. (LOC.)

This print depicts the invasion of Gunpowder, Maryland, when Rebel forces captured a train on July 11, 1864. On that day, Confederate colonel Harry W. Gilmor led a daring raid on the Philadelphia, Wilmington & Baltimore Railroad near Gunpowder, Maryland (near present-day Joppatowne). During the raid, supplies and horses were captured, and all passengers were forced to exit the train before it was set on fire. The event would be famously known as Gilmor's Raid. (LOC.)

Gen. Joseph Hooker's division camped during the winter near Mattawomen Creek, Maryland, most likely on land that today is known as Stump Neck Annex. In this March 1862 print by famed special artist Arthur Lumley, soldiers of the 8th New Jersey Volunteers are shown chopping wood and preparing branches to be used as firewood. Shortly after this print was sketched, the division would march toward Williamsburg, Virginia, where they would participate in the Peninsula Campaign. (LOC.)

The United States Christian Commission was an organization whose establishment came from a convention of Young Men's Christian Association (YMCA) leaders in New York City. The organization provided supplies, medical services, and religious books and literature to the troops in the field. This photograph shows one of the Christian Commission camp headquarters near Germantown, Maryland. At Antietam, the Christian Commission was headquartered on the Susan Hoffman farm. A volunteer, James Grant, arrived in the midst of the battle and found that every room in the building, the yard, and surrounding fields were filled with injured soldiers. Another civilian aid organization at Antietam was the United States Sanitary Commission. Headquartered along with the Christian Commission, they distributed supplies to the wounded and their caretakers. (NARA.)

Four

HOSPITALS AND
PRISONERS OF WAR

In Maryland, the Civil War resulted in numerous wounded soldiers needing care and large numbers of prisoners of war. In the Union army, each regiment had its own hospital responsible for its soldiers. In the battlefield, medical care usually came in the form of field hospitals that would temporarily occupy a nearby building or tent. The Union also had general hospitals, which were set up to care for the most serious of injuries, soldiers requiring extended periods of recovery and long-term care. This was generally the case for the most severely injured received during prisoners-of-war exchanges.

Maryland was home to numerous general hospitals, with locations including the US Naval Academy, Patterson Park in Baltimore, Annapolis Junction, and Point Lookout. Hammond General Hospital at Point Lookout, Maryland, was originally built to support the soldiers at Point Lookout. Later, when a prisoner-of-war camp was built near the hospital, it began supporting the vast numbers of Confederate prisoners of war.

A Confederate prisoner-of-war camp was built at Point Lookout in 1863. The camp, originally configured to support up to 10,000 prisoners, would be processing as many as 20,000 prisoners after the Battle at Gettysburg. The conditions at the camp soon became deplorable as there was not enough potable water to support the vast numbers of Union and Confederate soldiers. Prisoners were left to sleep 8 to 10 in a single tent, which provided very little protection against the pounding winds the area received during the winter months. Food was soon rationed, and prisoners began to suffer from malnutrition. By the summer of 1864, as many as 15 prisoners were dying each day. When the war ended and the camp closed, nearly 4,000 documented prisoners had died and were buried nearby. Some historians believe the actual number of Confederates that died at Point Lookout is closer to 10,000.

After the US Naval Academy was moved to Newport, Rhode Island, the grounds of the former academy at Annapolis were occupied by Union troops as a military encampment and general hospital. US General Hospital, Division No. 1 was organized and immediately utilized many of the existing academy buildings. Tents, shown in this print, were later set up when overcrowding after the Battle at Gettysburg became an issue. (HRC.)

After the Battle at Antietam, special artist Edwin Forbes sketched this print showing how area farmhouses in and around the battleground were used as temporary hospitals. In this sketch from September 18, 1862, a local farmhouse is used as a hospital by the Confederates. Lying on the ground nearby are their dead and wounded. Only 22 years old when the war started, Forbes was best known for sketching the day-to-day life of soldiers during the Civil War. (LOC.)

Taken in 1864, this photograph shows wounded officers relaxing at the US General Hospital, Division No. 1 in Annapolis, Maryland. They are, from left to right, Capt. J.L. Johnson (120th Pennsylvania Volunteer Infantry), 1st Lt. Philip E. Chapin (2nd Connecticut Artillery), Lt. Col. Nathan Goff Jr. (22nd US Colored Troops), Maj. P.B. Wilson (2nd Pennsylvania Volunteers), Lt. Col. Charles E. Stanton (21st Connecticut Volunteers), assistant surgeon H.A. Manchlin (United States Volunteers), and Maj. E.W. Payne (106th New York Volunteers). (HRC.)

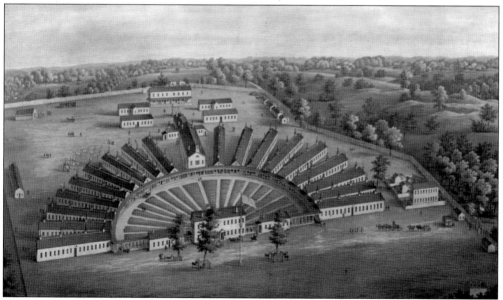

Hicks US General Hospital, located in Baltimore, was completed in June 1865 but was barely used as the war had ended just two months earlier. In 1866, one year after the war ended, lumber from Hicks US General Hospital was acquired by the Freedman's Bureau and sent to the Baltimore Association for the Moral and Educational Improvement of Colored People. This Baltimore Association was formed by Baltimore businessmen, clergymen, and lawyers who sought to educate the recently emancipated black population of Maryland. The lumber from Hicks US General Hospital was used to build more than 60 schoolhouses in Maryland. (LOC.)

The flag-of-truce boat *New York*, shown here anchored at Annapolis, was used to transfer recently paroled Union troops. In the photograph above, troops arrive at the US Naval Academy from where they would then be marched to Camp Parole, where they would be assigned until being officially paroled and either returned to their units or sent home. Typically, an arriving boat would contain more than 400 former prisoners of war. Initially, there were no medical personnel onboard the flag-of-truce boats, which resulted in some malnutrition or injured soldiers dying during transport. However, a subsequent recommendation from the commissary general of prisons would have such personnel on the boat when the prisoners were first exchanged so that immediate care could be given to the most severe of injuries. (Both, HRC.)

Union prisoners recently released from the Confederate prisons known as Belle Isle Prison and Libby Prison were sent to College Green Barracks, where they received initial medical treatment. Col. William Hoffman, commissary general of prisons, noted, "They generally arrive in a state of extreme destitution, with little or no clothing and that covered with filth and vermin." Soldiers such as these that suffered from malnutrition, long-term illnesses, and severe wounds were then admitted to the military hospital at the Naval Academy, where they were attended to by a group of more than 20 female nurses. Each nurse could be responsible for as many as 100 soldiers in her care. The nurses would read soldiers' letters from home or help them write messages to their awaiting families. Once released from the Naval Academy hospital, the men would be returned to Camp Parole and would either be reunited with their military unit or mustered out of the military. (Both, LOC.)

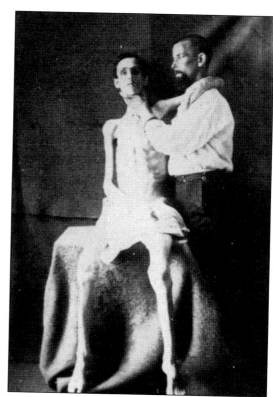

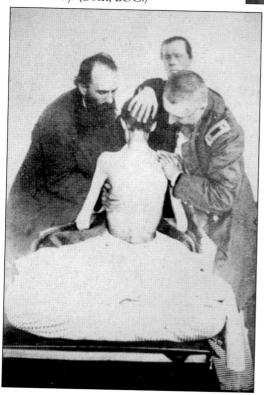

Camp Parole was set up outside of Annapolis to process Union prisoners of war who were paroled in prisoner exchanges between the North and South. Paroled prisoners would arrive at the Annapolis wharf via flag-of-truce boats from locations like City Point, Virginia. These ships would carry from several hundred to several thousand soldiers. This camp was located in what is now the Annapolis suburb of Parole, Maryland. At one time, as many as 70,000 soldiers were

processed at the camp. In April 1864, when negotiations broke down over the South's refusal to release captured black Union soldiers, Gen. Ulysses S. Grant stopped the exchange of prisoners. During this time, activities at Camp Parole diminished. Prisoner exchanges would resume again in January 1865. (LOC.)

This print shows St. John's College in Annapolis, Maryland, which was taken over by the military during the war. Many colleges suffered reduced enrollment as young men rushed to join and fight for their cause. Three of St. John's College Green Barracks buildings, originally constructed for the

Pennsylvania 67th Regiment Volunteers, were used to receive the newly arrived Union parolees and could accommodate up to 150 men per structure. US General Hospital, Division No. 2 would provide immediate care to soldiers before they were transferred to Camp Parole. (HRC.)

HEADQUARTERS FOR THE GENERAL COMMANDING
ST. MARYS DISTRICT

POINT LOOKO...
VIEW OF HAMMOND GEN! HOSPITAL & U.S. GEN!

1.	Light house,	7.	Chapel,	13.	Ward E.
2.	Dining room & kitchen,	8.	Reservoir,	14.	E. L. Donnellys Store,
3.	Hospital Headquarters,	9.	Clerk of wards,	15.	Dead house,
4.	Baggage house,	10.	Ward C.	16.	Sisters' quarters.
5.	Reading room,	11.	" D.	17.	Wharf & Post - Com. buildings,
6.	Half Diet kitchen,	12.	" F.	18.	Ice house.

34.	Line dividing Hospt. fr. Military.	40.	Office of Com. of Musters	45.	Convalescent quarters.	50.	Qrs. M'Col. Bailey 2nd, N. H.
35.	Qrs. of Capt. L欧欧se, C. S.	41.	Office of Capt. Pattersons Provost Marshal.	46.	Star Spangled Masonic Lodge,	51.	Camp of 2nd, N. H. V.
36.	" of Mr Tompkins a. m. Clerk.			47.	Murphy's farm house,	52.	" of 12th, N. H. V.
37.	Qrs. of Capt. Cook C. S.	42.	Brig. Gen. Martons Headquarters	48.	Hospital 2nd N. H. V.	53.	Qrs. of Major Langley, Com. 12th, N. H. V.
38.	" of Lt. Surgeon Ord. officer,	43.	2nd Wisconsin battery,	49.	Qrs. of Dr. Morrow, Sur. 2nd N. H. V.	
39.	" of Capt. Godfrey, Q. M.	44.	Cluster of stables,			

PRISONERS OF WAR.

This print, sketched in 1863, shows Hammond General Hospital (the spoke-like, circular building located in the lower left), the prisoner-of-war camp, and other military encampments constructed at Point Lookout. The prisoner camp was surrounded by a 14-foot-high wall and platform from which guards would perform sentry duty. More than 50,000 prisoners passed through the camp over the course of the war, and though it was originally built to hold only 10,000 men, it would eventually hold upwards of 20,000 at a time until prisoner exchanges were halted for a period. The National Park Service owns and operates this land today and estimates that more than 3,800 Confederate soldiers died and were buried at Point Lookout. A Confederate cemetery monument and obelisk marks the location of a single mass-burial location where soldiers' remains were interred. (LOC.)

During the war, the Point Lookout prisoner-of-war complex had a dock on the west side of the grounds, just north of the Hammond General Hospital. Supply boats would off-load their sundries to support the large contingent of soldiers and prisoners. In this wartime photograph, a large number of supply boats are seen anchored at the dock. (HRC.)

E.S. Bronson was the acting assistant surgeon at the Small Pox General Hospital located north of the prisoner-of-war camp at Point Lookout. The small facility (identified as No. 60 in the print on pages 66 and 67) consisted of a house and tents and could support a capacity of 100. Over the course of the war, the hospital attended to thousands of Union and Confederate patients. (HRC.)

Maria L. Poole was a nurse at Hammond General Hospital, located at Point Lookout, Maryland. Prior to the Civil War, most nurses in the Army were male. However, that would change after the appointment of Dorothea Dix as superintendent of army nurses. Dix would set strict guidelines for nurse candidates, including requirements that nurses had to be between 35 and 50 years old, be plain looking, and wear no jewelry or cosmetics. (HRC.)

Judson Gilman served as the acting assistant surgeon at Hammond General Hospital from 1863 to 1865. Born in Meredith, New Hampshire, in 1818, Gilman attended the University of Maryland and settled in Baltimore in 1845. At the outbreak of the war, he volunteered and was assigned to the Maryland 5th Infantry Regiment, where he served from 1861 to 1863. He died at Baltimore on August 1, 1883, at the age of 65. (HRC.)

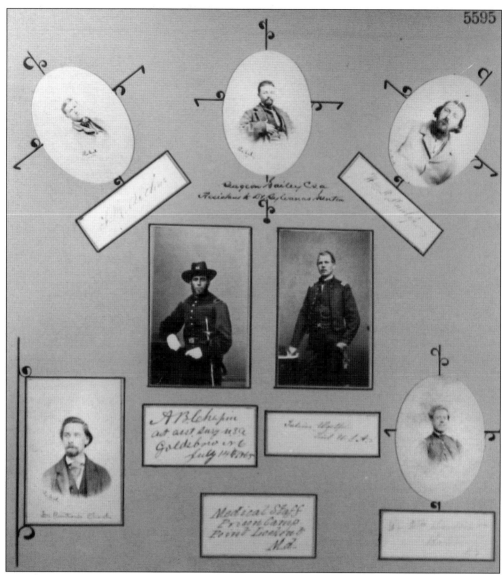

The medical staff at the Point Lookout prisoners-of-war camp consisted of both Union and Confederate personnel. Over the course of the war, they would support the Hammond General Hospital, the camp detainees, and the Union soldiers assigned to the Point Lookout area that supported and protected the encampments. Shown in this photograph are, from left to right, assistant surgeon F.M. Arthur (Confederacy), surgeon Bailey (Confederacy), assistant surgeon William D. Dunlap (Confederacy), unidentified soldier, acting assistant surgeon A.B. Chapin (Union), Lt. Julius Woelfel (Union), and surgeon William Broadbent (Confederacy). (HRC.)

In these photographs, members of the 5th Massachusetts Colored Cavalry Regiment are shown near their quarters at Point Lookout. In the photograph below are, from left to right, (seated) Capt. F. Higginson, Capt. J. Anderson, Capt. C. Emery, 2nd Lt. H. Hinckley, Maj. H. Bowditch, Capt. C. Allan, Maj. Z. Adams, Capt. H. Clark, and 1st Lt. E. Adams; (standing) Capt. F. Gilman, 1st Lt. J. Fisher, 1st Lt. Adjt. D. Chamberlain, unidentified, 1st Lt. G. Odell, unidentified, 2nd Lt. E. Bartlett, 1st Lt. C. Wheeler, unidentified, unidentified ladies in doorway, two unidentified, 1st Lt. A. Swain, two unidentified, 1st Lt. A. Mallory, 1st Lt. J. White, 1st Lt. R. Loud, unidentified, and 2nd Lt. R. Oliver. (Both, HRC.)

Annapolis Junction, Maryland, was not only the location and headquarters of regiments guarding the railroads between Washington, Annapolis, and Baltimore, it was also the site of Rulison Army General Hospital. In the print above, the Howard House Hotel is shown on the left, and the Annapolis Junction Hotel is shown on the right. Rulison General Hospital, built in 1863, was a sprawling complex, with its primary road being today's Main Street in Annapolis Junction. In the photograph below, plans for Rulison show the hospital to be built opposite the Howard Hotel and behind the Annapolis Junction Hotel. When finished, Rulison would include a total of nine wards and support up to 290 beds. (Above, courtesy of LOC; below, courtesy US National Institute of Health.)

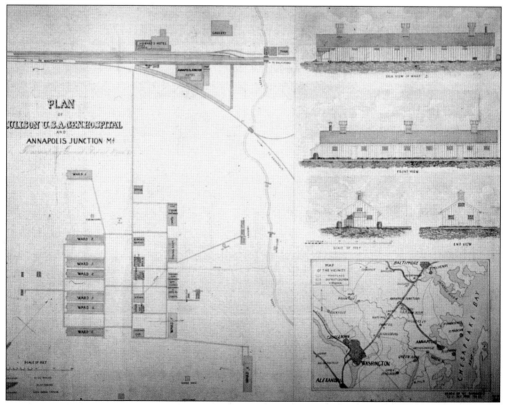

The Smith family barn shown in the photograph above, located in Keedysville, Maryland, was used as a field hospital after the Battle of Antietam. Due to the large number of casualties, nearly all buildings in vicinity were used to treat the wounded. In the photograph below, surgeon Anson Hurd of the 14th Indiana Infantry attends to Confederate wounded on the Smiths' farm. Dr. Hurd enlisted and was commissioned in the 14th Indiana on April 21, 1862. Five months later, he was witness to the devastation at the Battle of Antietam. He would resign his commission just three months later. (Both, LOC.)

Hessian Barracks, located in Frederick, Maryland, was used as a hospital after the Battle of Antietam. More than 4,000 wounded were brought to Frederick after the fighting. Built in 1780, the barracks is a stone, *L*-shaped structure with a gable roof and gallery porches. During the Colonial period, the barracks had functioned as a prison. Later, from 1853 until 1860, the barracks were used as an agricultural fairgrounds. Shortly after the war, the buildings and grounds were chosen as the new home to the Maryland School for the Deaf. (HRC.)

Five

BUILDINGS AND HOMES
OF THE PERIOD

Photography was in its infancy at the start of the Civil War. The average citizen could not afford the luxury of it because the materials used in producing the images were too expensive. Therefore, the majority of photographs of buildings prior to the war were usually from the major cities where photographers had set up their shops. The Civil War would change that when traveling photographers would move with the military units, capturing the after-battle scenes for historical record.

At Antietam, Alexander Gardner and his assistant would take hundreds of photographs of the devastation of war. Because the battles were fought in the populated areas like Sharpsburg and Boonsboro, the images would naturally capture some of the buildings and structures lived in and used by the local farming communities. When families deserted their homes for safer ground away from the impending battle, the military would occupy their homesteads and use them for command headquarters, officers' quarters, and field hospitals. Livestock and crops were simply taken by the military and used to feed the soldiers. After the war, farmers would have to file claims for losses and damage to their property. Rarely would a farmer receive full compensation for their losses. In many cases, farmers and business owners simply lost everything they had to sustain their families and businesses.

After the war, historians and preservationists would spend countless hours reviewing the images for every minute detail. The photographs taken at the battlefields would serve a purpose other than documenting the devastation; they would also provide preservationists with exacting detail on the construction and buildings of the period. When the National Park Service began acquiring the land where the battles had taken place and wanted to make them into national parks, the photographs would again be used to aid in preserving and recreating the buildings, fences, and farmlands of the war period.

Local residents of Cumberland, Maryland, patiently await news about the April 19, 1861, Baltimore Riots at the local bookstore and news depot. Like many Marylanders, the reaction in Cumberland was mixed, with support for both sides of the war. After hearing of the news and seeing the reaction by local residents, a local paper printed, "From this time forward the lines became more closely drawn, and friends and neighbors were unhappily arrayed one against the other." Cumberland was a large Union stronghold during the war as numerous federal troops were garrisoned nearby to protect the vital B&O Railroad from Confederate raiders. A small cavalry engagement occurred west of Cumberland, near Folck's Mill, on August 1, 1864, when recently mustered Union cavalry troops dueled with Confederate cavalry. (LOC.)

This photograph of Baltimore Street in downtown Cumberland was taken in April 1862, shortly after a snowstorm. Cumberland was routinely raided during the Civil War by Confederates attempting to disrupt the B&O Railroad. The Revere House hotel, seen on the right in the photograph, became famous in February 1865 when Union general George Crook was kidnapped there by Confederate lieutenant Jesse McNeill's raiders while he slept. The building is no longer standing, but a historical marker located near the site recognizes McNeill's Raid. McNeill became famous for his daring raids and was the target of Union brigadier general Benjamin F. Kelley. After one such raid, Kelley wrote, "As soon as practicable send Captain Hart with 125 or 150 men after McNeill . . . I will simply say I want McNeill killed." (LOC.)

The Maryland Agricultural College, pictured here in 1865, was founded by Charles Benedict Calvert and opened in October 1859. When the war broke out, many students resigned to join the fighting. The college would suffer during the war and would close its doors in 1866 because of a lack of funding. In 1920, the college would become known as the University of Maryland. (LOC.)

St. Joseph's College in Emmitsburg, Maryland, became host to numerous Union units prior to the Battle of Gettysburg. The 5th Michigan Cavalry camped on the grounds on June 27, 1863. A few days later, a company of Signal Corps was directed by General Reynolds to set up a signal station behind the college on Catoctin Mountain near Indian Lookout. (LOC.)

Mount St. Mary's College in Emmitsburg, pictured here in July 1863, is the oldest independent Catholic college in the United States. Like many of the Maryland colleges at the start of the war, Mount St. Mary's had both students and faculty that supported each side of the war. (LOC.)

This photograph of the Farmers & Drovers Inn located in Emmitsburg was taken in early July 1863. On July 5, 1863, seventy Union soldiers and one of Mathew Brady's "special artists" were captured here by Confederate general J.E.B. Stuart. The building still exists today and is known as the Emmit House. A third floor was added in 1875. (LOC.)

The badly damaged Lutheran church on Main Street in Sharpsburg, Maryland, stood on Cemetery Hill. Confederate signal officers used the steeple as a signal tower during the battle, and immediately afterward the structure was used as a hospital for the wounded. The building was damaged beyond repair and, after the war, had to be torn down. The materials from this church were then used to repair other churches in the community. (LOC.)

After the Battle of Antietam, General McClellan selected the Lee house in Pleasant Valley, Maryland, as a temporary home for his wife. Here, officers of the Army of the Potomac were to have been photographed with General McClellan, but the general had to leave just as Alexander Gardner was about to take the picture. The McClellans stayed in the house well into October 1862. (LOC.)

These photographs of Sharpsburg, Maryland, were taken by Alexander Gardner shortly after the Battle of Antietam in September 1862. St. Paul's Episcopal Church can be seen in both views. Above, the church is visible to the left. This photograph appears to have been taken looking north down present-day Hall Street. Below, looking west down Main Street, the church can be seen in the distance on the right. The original building was so damaged by the war that it had to be torn down. Its original stones and bell were used in the construction of a new church, which was moved forward on the lot and closer to Main Street. (Both, LOC.)

The David R. Miller family sits on the front porch of their home on Hagerstown Pike. This photograph was taken around 1870, several years after the Antietam battle. The Miller cornfield was the scene of devastating weapons fire as both men and corn stalks were cut down where they stood. After the war, David Miller received only $995 from the government for losses of forage and horses and damages to the house. (LOC.)

Two days before the Battle of Antietam, Samuel and Elizabeth Mumma took their 13 children and left for safety. When they returned on September 19, 1862, they found that their house and barn had been burned. Confederate soldiers had destroyed the buildings so that they could not be used by Union sharpshooters. In this photograph, unidentified people appear to be inspecting the damages. (LOC.)

The William and Margaret Roulette home and farm, shown in this photograph by Alexander Gardner, became key ground for the fighting at Antietam. The barn was used as a field hospital, and more than 700 dead were buried in fields on the property. Beehives seen in the front yard of this photograph were knocked over by an artillery shell, causing chaos among the fighting troops. (LOC.)

The Reel family barn, located in Sharpsburg, Maryland, was burned to the ground when a Federal artillery shell hit it and started a fire. In this photograph taken after the battle, all that remains is the stone shell of the former barn. The 1860 census shows that Henry Reel (spelled "Real" in the census) lived on the farm with his wife, Barbara, and their children Melvin, Josephine, Ida, and John. (LOC.)

Joseph and Sarah Sherrick lived in this house near Burnside's Bridge at Antietam, Maryland. Confederate troops from Brigadier General Toombs's brigade set up positions around the Sherrick home on the morning of the battle. Very little damage was done to the structure, but the dead from both armies were strewn about the Sherrick property. (LOC.)

Gen. George McClellan took over the Philip Pry farm and home to use as his headquarters during the battle. Gen. Israel Richardson was taken to the house after being wounded during the battle at Bloody Lane. During his visit to Antietam, President Lincoln visited Richardson at the Pry house. Richardson would die in an upstairs bedroom on November 3, 1862. (LOC.)

Joshua Newcomer owned and operated this mill at Sharpsburg, Maryland. After the battle, his house and the mill would be used by the Federal army to care for the wounded. Like many other nearby farmers and business owners, Newcomer would file a claim against the government to be compensated for goods used by the soldiers. Unable to rebound from the losses, he eventually sold the house and mill. (LOC.)

On July 12, 1864, all that remained of Montgomery Blair's Silver Spring mansion was the burned shell of its former self. Soldiers under Confederate general Jubal Early ransacked, looted, and then burned the house after arriving near the Fort Stevens breastworks on July 11. The home, called Falkland, was built in the 1850s and was occupied by the son of the founder of Silver Spring. Pres. Abraham Lincoln and wife Mary personally witnessed the fighting from the Fort Stevens parapets. Early would later be quoted as saying, "Major, we didn't take Washington but we scared Abe Lincoln like hell." (LOC.)

Probably the most famous building at Antietam is the Dunker Church. Built by local Dunker farmers in 1852, the small church had only about six families in the congregation. The Dunkers are a Bretheren group similar to the Amish or Mennonites with a history that originated in Germany in the early 1700s. The land for the church was donated to the Dunkers by Samuel Mumma. During the Battle of Antietam, numerous Union attacks against Confederate forces occurred in the general area of the structure. On the morning following the battle, the Confederates used the church as a field hospital. One account states that a truce occurred on the evening of September 18 at the Dunker Church so that opposing sides could exchange the wounded and bury their dead. Years later, as reunions would occur at Antietam, it was not uncommon for symbolic photographs to be taken at the famous church. (LOC.)

Six

BRIDGES AND RAILROADS
OF THE WAR

Bridges and railroads played an important role in the Civil War in Maryland. As the military battles moved from city to city and across state lines, existing bridges would be used or temporary pontoon bridges would be constructed. The military teams responsible for building the pontoon bridges became so efficient that they could construct one in hours if needed. This was certainly the case when Confederate general Robert E. Lee was trapped at Williamsport, Maryland, and his men built a bridge and escaped into Virginia in the middle of the night.

At Antietam, several bridges would become key factors in the results of some battles. Three stone bridges (known as "Lower," "Middle," and "Upper" to local residents) would play prominent roles in the photographs taken by Alexander Gardner. Of the three, the Middle Bridge is the only one not still standing today. Located on the main road (Route 34) leading into Sharpsburg, it was destroyed by floodwaters in 1889 and was later replaced by a more modern bridge.

The railroads of the period were used to transport men, supplies, ammunition, and prisoners of war. The Confederates would employ raid tactics to destroy the tracks and railcars in order to slow down military movements. At the start of the war, Union commanders noted that the rail lines between Baltimore and Washington were crucial to protecting Washington and keeping communication lines open. Regimental guards were placed up and down the rail lines, and pickets guarded the tracks around the clock.

President Lincoln used the railroads when he traveled to Antietam and Gettysburg to view the battlefields. He traveled through Annapolis Junction and Relay, Maryland, where he changed trains. His final trip on the railroad came after his assassination, when his coffin traveled on a special funeral train from Washington, DC, through Baltimore, Philadelphia, Harrisburg, New York, and Chicago before finally arriving at its destination of Springfield, Illinois.

The Union Arch Bridge, today known as the Cabin John Bridge, was built by Gen. M.C. Meigs and designed by Alfred L. Rives as part of the Washington Aqueduct and as a roadway bridge. Construction began in 1857 and was completed in 1864. The bridge was 450 feet long and had a single arch span of 220 feet. The arch ring was constructed of granite quarried in Quincy, Massachusetts, while the remainder of the granite came from a newly dug quarry just a few hundred feet from the construction site. These photographs show a couple of views of the construction of the Union Arch Bridge. The photograph above was taken on February 27, 1861, and the photograph below was taken on August 12, 1861. Note the rolling carriages at the top of the scaffolding; these were used to move and place the heavy stones. (Both, LOC.)

At the outbreak of the Civil War, controversy ensued over the commemorative stone tablets to be attached to the bridge. Jefferson Davis, the secretary of war before the conflict, had his name inscribed on one of the tablets, but it was chiseled off shortly after the start of the war. Davis's name would eventually be restored in 1909 as a result of Southern lobbying of Pres. Theodore Roosevelt. In the photograph below, men are seen standing and sitting on top of the bridge while others gaze at it near the Cabin John Creek. As can be seen with the men hanging their legs over the side, the original bridge had no parapet. A railing was added in 1872 to make the bridge safer for roadway traffic. (Above, courtesy of NARA; below, courtesy of LOC.)

When possible, military units would use existing bridges to cross waterways. However, when the bridges had been destroyed by the enemy or when no bridge existed, pontoon bridges were used to cross rivers and large bodies of water. The photograph above is of a single pontoon being transported on a wagon and pulled by a team of up to six horses. These pontoons would be placed in the water and lashed together. The construction of the bridge would be accomplished with an abutment crew, a boat crew, a lashing crew, a chess crew, and a side-rail crew. The photograph below shows a completed pontoon bridge across the Potomac River at Berlin, Maryland. The pontoon teams were so efficient that one Union team of 450 men built a 2,200-foot-long pontoon across the James River in just five hours. (Both, NARA.)

The bridge at Berlin (now Brunswick), Maryland, pictured in these photographs, was destroyed in 1861 by Confederate forces. Alexander Gardner took the photograph above in October 1862, shortly after the Battle of Antietam. All that remains of the bridge are the stone piers. In the photograph below, taken about two weeks after the Battle at Gettysburg, General Meade's army is shown camped near the stone ruins of the Berlin Bridge where two pontoon bridges were built to cross the Potomac. The original caption attached to this photograph, "The leisurely pursuit," was a reference to Meade's failure to destroy Lee's Army of Northern Virginia when it most vulnerable and his subsequent slow pursuit. President Lincoln would later chastise Meade for not attacking Lee when he had the chance. (Both, LOC.)

At the time of the Civil War, standard photography was unable to capture moving objects without the image being blurred. During the war, special artists were used by newspapers to capture these moving objects by sketching them. Edwin Forbes sketched these two scenes at Antietam, Maryland. In the print above, he captures the moment when General Burnside's division crossed the Middle Bridge at Antietam and stormed the Rebel positions on the other side. After the Battle at Gettysburg, General Meade pursued General Lee's forces from Pennsylvania through western Maryland, where numerous battles and skirmishes took place at Williamsport, Boonsboro, and Funkstown. In the print below, Forbes depicts the moment when some of Meade's forces successfully crossed the Antietam Bridge. Meade's remaining forces were held off at Sharpsburg when they encountered Confederate cavalry brigades. (Both, LOC.)

These photographs of the Middle Bridge at Antietam were taken shortly after the battle. The image above is from September 22, 1862, just five days after the heavy fighting had subsided, and shows two ladies enjoying a picnic in a boat. One man holds the horse and buggy while the other is stirring something for one of the ladies. The ladies are holding what appear to be hardtacks—crackers or biscuits eaten by Civil War soldiers when no other food was available. The photograph below was taken from higher ground and provides an excellent view across the bridge. The boat used by the young ladies in the photograph above can be seen in the photograph below at the base of the bridge. (Both, LOC.)

These photographs look across the Middle Bridge on the Sharpsburg and Boonsboro Turnpike at Antietam, Maryland. The photograph above was taken from the east side of the bridge with a southwesterly view. The Newcomer Farm and barn can be seen in the upper left portion of the image. The barn and portions of the mill are visible on the opposite side of the bridge in the photograph below. The bridge, sometimes referred to as the "Newcomer Bridge," was originally known as the Orndorff Bridge. Christopher Orndorff built the Newcomer home in the 1780s. The Middle Bridge was destroyed by flooding in 1889 and no longer exists, though a historical marker today identifies its original location. (Both, LOC.)

The Middle Bridge area of Antietam was highly photographed by Alexander Gardner. The photograph above was taken from the Newcomer Mill side of the bridge. Looking closely, one can see a boat just above the small waterfall on the right side of the photograph; this is the boat used by the ladies in the upper photograph on page 93. The photograph below was taken from the northeastern side of the Middle Bridge at the edge of the creek. This image provides a good view of the high ridge opposite the Newcomer Mill. Cornfields can be seen at the top of the ridge. (Both, LOC.)

Undoubtedly the most famous bridge in Maryland during the Civil War was the Burnside Bridge. Originally known as the Lower Bridge, it was named after Maj. Gen. Ambrose Burnside. During the Battle of Antietam, Confederate soldiers from Georgia managed to hold off Union advances on the bridge for nearly four hours. Eventually, Federal soldiers led by General Burnside took the bridge. In the photograph above, two wooden barrels are seen in the Antietam Creek days after the battle. These barrels were typically used by the armies to store gunpowder, food, and water. Alexander Gardner took these photographs, and his mobile photographic wagon is seen below, near the bridge. (Both, LOC.)

Burnside Bridge at Antietam became so famous for the Georgia Rebels' ability to hold the bridge for several hours and for Burnside's charge to take it that it was photographed numerous times. Mathew Brady sent two photographers to Antietam—Alexander Gardner and his assistant James Gibson. The majority of the photographs at Antietam were taken by Gardner, and these images of Burnside Bridge were taken by both Gardner and Gibson from nearly the same position on the southeast side of Burnside Bridge. The photograph above was taken by Gardner, probably in early afternoon, based upon the shadows cast by the trees. The photograph below was taken by Gibson. (Both, LOC.)

Confederate raiders continued to destroy railroads and communications lines in Maryland throughout the war. On July 11, 1864, about 125 men from Gilmor's Raiders came upon several trains at the Philadelphia, Wilmington & Baltimore Railroad Magnolia Station near Gunpowder, Maryland, and destroyed them, along with the nearby Gunpowder Creek Bridge. On board one of the train cars was US major general Franklin dressed in civilian clothes. He had hoped to not be recognized by the Confederate raiders; however, a Southern spy was also on the train and quickly identified the general to Captain Gilmor. Franklin was apprehended but would escape from his captors later that night while they slept. US mail pouches onboard the train cars were opened up and strewn all along the ground and passengers were forced off the train before raiders began setting the train cars on fire and then moving them onto the bridge. One soldier would later write that upon arriving at the burned station via a train from the north and after witnessing the passengers reading the strewn US mail, he crossed the burnt bridge along planks that had already been replaced by workmen repairing the bridge and proceeded south on a train waiting on the other side of the tracks. (LOC.)

HEAD QUARTERS

RAILROAD BRIGADE

Relay House, 17th March, 1862.

General Order,
NO. 18.

Every Officer and all Pickets of the Brigade will, when required,

GIVE AID AND ASSISTANCE

To Conductors on the Railroad,

To Preserve Order in the Trains; and to Apprehend and Retain in Custody any Disorderly Person guilty of Infraction of Law,

To be dealt with as a Court may determine; the circumstance to be reported to these Head Quarters without delay.

D. S. MILES,
Col. 2d Inf., Comdg. R. R. Brigade.

This is a broadside poster of General Order No. 18, which gave soldiers of the Railroad Brigade at the Relay House the authority to arrest any suspicious travelers suspected of breaking any law. Over the course of the war, numerous citizens were arrested at the Relay House for concealing or attempting to transport goods, ammunition, and blast caps to Confederate forces in the South. Col. Dixon S. Miles, commander of the Railroad Brigade in March 1862, was born in Baltimore and fought at the First Battle of Bull Run. During the Antietam Campaign, he commanded the Harpers Ferry Garrison. He was wounded at Harpers Ferry the day before the Battle of Antietam and died that night. (B&O.)

Annapolis Junction served an important role in the Civil War. The small town supported a regiment of guards protecting the railroad lines from Washington to Baltimore, and it also hosted a general hospital complex. Before the war, the Howard House Hotel and the Annapolis Junction Hotel provided a stopover location for travelers. In this photograph taken after the war and looking north toward Baltimore, the Howard House Hotel is seen on the left and the Annapolis Junction hotel can be seen on the right. When comparing this photograph against the artistic print of the complex on page 72 of this book, it is amazing how accurate the artist was in his capturing the details of the structures and railroad. The Howard House Hotel would have been located very near to where the former Henkel's Restaurant existed some years ago. (B&O.)

In this c. 1930 photograph of the Annapolis Junction area, it is evident that the Annapolis Junction Hotel no longer exists. The tracks for the now abandoned Annapolis & Elk Ridge Railroad can be seen behind the train station, which was located at the wye split of the tracks. This rail line operated until about 1935, and a portion of the line continued to support Fort Meade and Odenton until around 1981. The building in the left of the photograph remained from the Civil War period and is shown in the print on page 72. It would have been located where Henkels Lane meets the B&O Railroad today. During the war, the Annapolis Junction area was the headquarters for a regiment of Railroad Brigade guards that patrolled the railroads from Washington to Baltimore to keep the supply routes and communication lines open to the capital. (B&O.)

The B&O Railroad Bridge crossing between Maryland Heights, Maryland, and Harpers Ferry, West Virginia, is shown in this picture dating to 1865. The wooden bridge, originally built around 1838, was destroyed by both Confederate and Union forces a total of four times during the course of the war. The last time was in July 1864 when Confederate general Jubal Early burned the structure while retreating from Maryland. The bridge was rebuilt again by October 1864. (LOC.)

The Lincoln funeral train, shown here at Philadelphia, Pennsylvania, left Washington, DC, on Friday, April 21, 1865. The train made stops at Annapolis Junction, Relay House, and Baltimore. In all, it would travel more than 1,650 miles, make stops in 13 major cities, and be honored by the citizens of six states and the District of Columbia. It was the first time the railroad was used to nationally commemorate the death of a US president. (B&O.)

Seven

THE LINCOLN ASSASSINATION

Many of the names of those involved in the events surrounding the assassination of Abraham Lincoln have long since been forgotten and are only footnotes in the history pages of the country's struggles. Many of the key players—like John Wilkes Booth, Mary Surratt, John Surratt, Edmund Spangler, and Dr. Samuel Mudd—lived in Maryland during the Civil War, a testament to the issues Maryland dealt with as a border state. Others, like Louis Weichmann and Reverdy Johnson, also had ties to Maryland and would play a part in the trial of the conspirators.

Conspiracy theories still abound today about the assassination of Abraham Lincoln. With digitization and easy access to documents from the period readily available online, researchers continue to shed more light on the other aspects of the assassination that never made it into the mainstream newspapers at the time or the schoolbooks of today. Even though nearly 150 years have passed since the events of April 15, 1865, historians still continue to review the massive number of war reports, police records, and other documents relating to the assassination. While Lincoln's murder would devastate a nation that was just beginning to heal from the wounds of war, the effects of the war and the abolishment of slavery in the United States would forever change the country for the good.

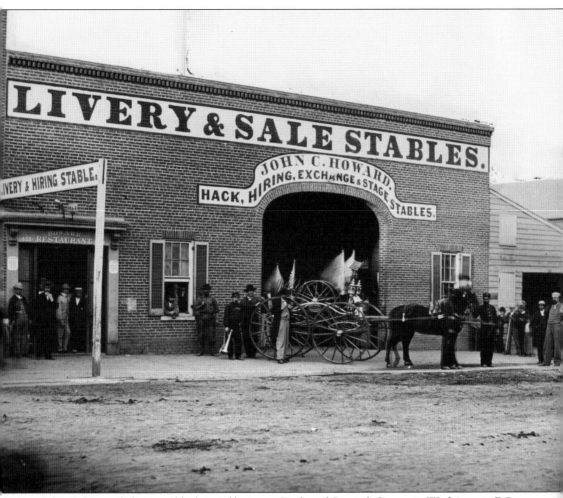

John C. Howard's horse stable, located between Sixth and Seventh Streets in Washington, DC, was used by both John Wilkes Booth and John Surratt during the Civil War. Brooke Stabler, operator of Howard's Livery Stable, testified before the conspiracy trial that John Surratt had sent a letter to him that said, "Mr. Howard will please let the bearer Mr. Atzerodt have my horse whenever he wishes to ride also my leggings and gloves and oblige." Surratt later sent another letter to Stabler on March 26, 1865, authorizing him to let Booth use his horse whenever he desired. Booth hired a horse from Howard's stable the day he assassinated Lincoln. This photograph, like many others relating to the assassination of Lincoln, was taken by Alexander Gardner. (LOC.)

This photograph of Ford's Theatre in Washington, DC, was taken in April 1865 after Lincoln's assassination. Military guards are visible at the entrance to the building. After the assassination, the theater remained closed until shortly after the hanging of the conspirators on July 7, 1865. On June 9, 1893, flooring of the theater gave way, and a front section of the building collapsed, killing 22 government employees. In 1933, the National Park Service took control of the building and called it the Lincoln Museum. Originally built in 1833 as a house of worship for the First Baptist Church of Washington, Ford's Theatre was destroyed by fire in 1862. It was rebuilt and reopened for business in August 1863 with a seating capacity of 2,400. Today, it is a museum and active theater. (LOC.)

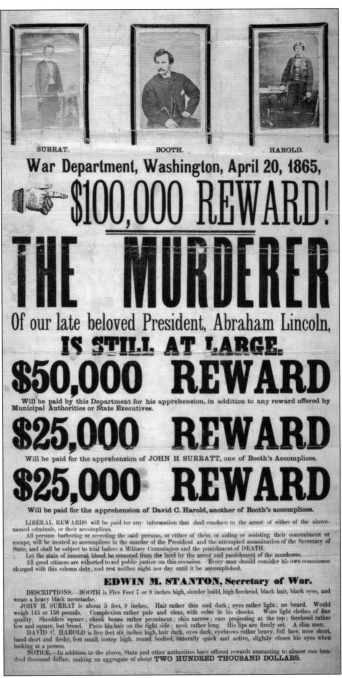

This broadside, published by the War Department immediately after Lincoln's assassination, identified the suspected accomplices: John Surratt, John Wilkes Booth, and David Herold. Herold was not well known at that time, resulting in his name being misspelled as Harold, as it is on this broadside. Later, more accomplices would be identified and sought after by the War Department. After the execution of the conspirators, claims would be settled on the reward money. In the end, more than 10 people received a portion of the reward, with Detective Conger receiving the most: $15,000. (LOC.)

John Wilkes Booth was a famous stage actor prior to the Civil War. Born in Bel Air, Maryland, on May 10, 1838, Booth played sports and was well liked. After assassinating Lincoln at Ford's Theatre, he would escape to Port Royal, Virginia, where he would be killed by a bullet from the gun of Sgt. Boston Corbett of the 16th New York Cavalry. (NARA.)

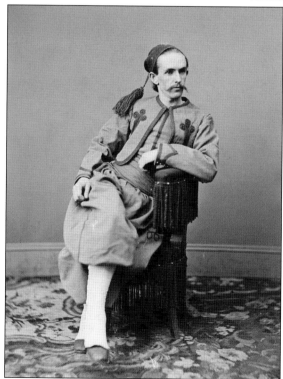

John H. Surratt Jr., born in Washington, DC, was identified as one of the Lincoln conspirators shortly after the assassination. During the Civil War, he worked for the Confederate Secret Service as a message courier and spy. After his capture overseas, he was brought back to Washington to stand trial. He was found not guilty of the charges against him and lived his last years near Baltimore, where he died on April 21, 1916, at the age of 72. (LOC.)

Lewis Powell was a conspirator in the plot to decapitate the Federal government in 1865. His role in the plot was to assassinate Secretary of State Seward while Booth went to Ford's Theatre to assassinate President Lincoln. After his capture, he was taken to the Washington Navy Yard and held onboard the USS *Saugus*. The photograph at left shows Powell wearing the same jacket and hat he had worn the night of his attempted assassination of Seward. In the photograph below, he is seen on the ironclad *Saugus* with his hands manacled. He was found guilty of the attempted murder of Seward and hanged on July 7, 1865, with the other conspirators. (Both, LOC.)

George Atzerodt met John Wilkes Booth in Washington, DC, and became a willing participant in the plan to kidnap Lincoln. Atzerodt later testified that he was assigned the task of assassinating Vice Pres. Andrew Johnson but could not find the courage to go through with it and began drinking at the hotel bar where Johnson lived. He was found guilty in the plot and hanged on July 7, 1865. (LOC.)

David Herold was an accomplice in the assassination of President Lincoln. After the attempted assassination of Seward, Herold and Powell split up. Herold crossed the Navy Yard Bridge and met up with Booth outside of Washington at Soper's Hill, about eight miles south of the city. They then escaped into Virginia, where they were eventually caught at the Garrett farm in Port Royal. Herold surrendered, and Booth was killed by Sgt. Boston Corbett. Herold was hanged on July 7, 1865, along with the other conspirators. (LOC.)

Mary Surratt was the mother of John and Anna Surratt and was a conspirator in the Lincoln assassination. She leased the family's Surratt's Tavern in Surrattsville, Maryland, and moved the family to Washington in October 1864. She would later be found guilty and hanged with the other conspirators on July 7, 1865, making her the first women to ever be executed by the federal government. (NARA.)

Edmund Spangler, who spent much of his adulthood in Baltimore, Maryland, was charged as a conspirator in the Lincoln plot and was found guilty. He served four years as a prisoner at Fort Jefferson in Dry Tortugas, Florida, along with three other lesser conspirators— Samuel Arnold, Michael O'Laughlen, and Dr. Samuel Mudd. (LOC.)

Samuel Arnold (right) and Michael O'Laughlen (below) were also involved in the plot to kidnap Abraham Lincoln in March 1865. When the plot failed, both men decided to have no more to do with the scheme. However, their names would forever be associated with Booth's because of testimony by John Surratt's friend Louis J. Weichmann. They would both be found guilty of participating in the plot and serve four years alongside Edmund Spangler and Dr. Samuel Mudd at Fort Jefferson. Spangler, Mudd, and Arnold were all pardoned by Pres. Andrew Johnson in 1869 and released. O'Laughlen died of yellow fever at Fort Jefferson in 1867 and was tended to during his last hours by Dr. Mudd. (Both, LOC.)

FREEDOM'S IMMORTAL TRIUMPH!

After the war, the North's vindictive feelings toward the South were evident in this print from late 1865. Marylander John Wilkes Booth is pictured in the lower right with Jefferson Davis hanging from a tree. Hangman's nooses are suspended over the heads of Gen. Robert E. Lee, Secretary of War John C. Breckinridge, Secretary of State and War Judah P. Benjamin, and others. The infamous Libby and Andersonville Prisons are shown in the background while an angelic Abraham Lincoln is led to heaving by angels. (LOC.)

Anna Surratt, the daughter of Mary Surratt and sister of John Surratt, played no part in the either the kidnapping plot or the assassination plot. She later married William P. Tonry, a chemist working for the surgeon general's office. Ironically, he worked at Ford's Theatre, which had been converted into government offices after Lincoln's assassination. (NARA.)

Edwin T. Booth, brother of Lincoln assassinator John Wilkes Booth, was a famous actor like his brother. Born in Bel Air, Maryland, Edwin took up acting like the rest of his famous family. He was not involved in any part of the plots to kidnap or assassinate Abraham Lincoln. However, after Lincoln's assassination, the Booth name would live in infamy. He would continue acting until his death on July 7, 1893, at the age of 59. (NARA.)

Capt. Edward P. Doherty was a Union Civil War officer with the 16th New York Cavalry assigned to the defense of Washington, DC. He is best known for assembling a detachment of 25 men to track down and capture John Wilkes Booth. For capturing Booth and Herold, Doherty would receive $5,250 and be promoted to captain. He died in 1897 and was buried in Arlington National Cemetery. (NARA.)

Sgt. Thomas P. "Boston" Corbett served in the Union army and was assigned to the team of men charged with tracking down and capturing John Wilkes Booth. Corbett and other men on the team found Booth and Herold trapped in a tobacco barn on the property of Richard Garrett. After Herold surrendered, Corbett saw Booth through a crack in the barn wall and fired a single shot that hit Booth in the neck. (NARA.)

Reverdy Johnson was born in Annapolis, Maryland, and served in the Maryland State Senate from 1821 to 1825. During the military tribunal of the Lincoln conspirators, he represented Mary Surratt. She was convicted and hung with three other conspirators on July 7, 1865. On February 10, 1876, Johnson fell at the Maryland Governor's Mansion and hit his head on the building's granite base. He died instantly and is buried in Green Mount Cemetery in Baltimore. (NARA.)

Lincoln's funeral train departed Washington, DC, and followed a route through more than 400 communities and seven different states. The train was called the *Lincoln Special*, and a portrait of the president was affixed above the cattle guard on the front of the engine. Lincoln's son Willie, who died in 1862 of typhoid fever, was disinterred in Washington, DC, and transported on the train with the president. Willie would be buried next to his father in the family plot in Springfield, Illinois. The photograph above shows the engine *Nashville* and was taken somewhere along the route to Springfield. Several engines were used to transport the president's body to Illinois. The photograph below is of the funeral car that carried the president's coffin. The famous car, called the *United States*, would be destroyed by a fire in 1911. (Both, LOC.)

Gen. John F. Hartranft was assigned the duty of guarding the conspirators at the US Arsenal Prison in Washington, DC, during their trials. Pictured here are, from left to right, (seated) Capt. R.A. Watts, Lt. Col. William H.H. McCall, Gen. John F. Hartranft, Col. L.A. Dodd, and Capt. Christian Rath; (standing) Lt. Col. George W. Frederick, Lt. D.H. Geissinger, and assistant surgeon George L. Porter. (LOC.)

This is a photograph of the military commission that tried and convicted the Lincoln conspirators. Pictured are, from left to right, (seated) Lt. Col. David R. Clendenin, Col. C.H. Tompkins, Brig. Gen. Albion P. Howe, Brig. Gen. James Ekin, Maj. Gen. David Hunter, Brig. Gen. Robert S. Foster, John A. Binham, and Brig. Gen. Joseph Holt; (standing) Brig. Gen. Thomas M. Harris, Maj. Gen. Lew Wallace, Maj. Gen. August V. Kautz, and Henry L. Burnett. (LOC.)

These photographs, taken by Alexander Gardner at the Arsenal Prison Yard on July 7, 1865, show the prisoners on the scaffolding, surrounded by the execution officials. Gen. John F. Hartranft ordered a detail of soldiers to perform guard duty at the prison on the morning of the hangings. Spectators can be seen in front of the scaffolding along with the soldiers standing in line. Behind the scaffolding, additional soldiers stand upon the wall and watch as the procedure unfolds. Above, General Hartranft reads the death warrant to the conspirators. Below, hoods and ropes are placed over their heads in final preparation for their execution. (Both, LOC.)

These two photographs capture the moments after the execution as the crowd of spectators begins to leave the prison yard. The photograph above was probably taken from a nearby rooftop. A spectator can be seen in the second-floor, middle window of the small building attached to the prison building. The photograph below appears to have been taken at nearly the same time, but from a window of the two-story building behind the soldiers that are standing in front of the scaffolding. Due to the size of the courtyard, tickets had to be issued to spectators in order to control the number of people. Today, the grounds of the former Arsenal Penitentiary are part of Fort McNair. Tennis courts are now located where the scaffolding would have stood in 1865. (Both, LOC.)

After the crowd of spectators left the courtyard, graves were dug to the right of the scaffolding. The conspirators were taken down and placed in pine boxes with their hoods still covering their heads. The boxes were buried in the shallow graves, where they stayed for two years. When changes were planned for the prison grounds, the remains of the conspirators were exhumed and returned to their families for reburial in family plots. (LOC.)

The Lincoln presidency would suffer the effects of four bloody years of war. During this time, Lincoln would have his photograph taken numerous times. This image, believed to be the last one of the president alive, was taken by Alexander Gardner on February 5, 1865, at Gardner's gallery in Washington. On April 14 of that year, John Wilkes Booth would shoot the president at Ford's Theatre in Washington, DC, and Lincoln would die the following morning. (LOC.)

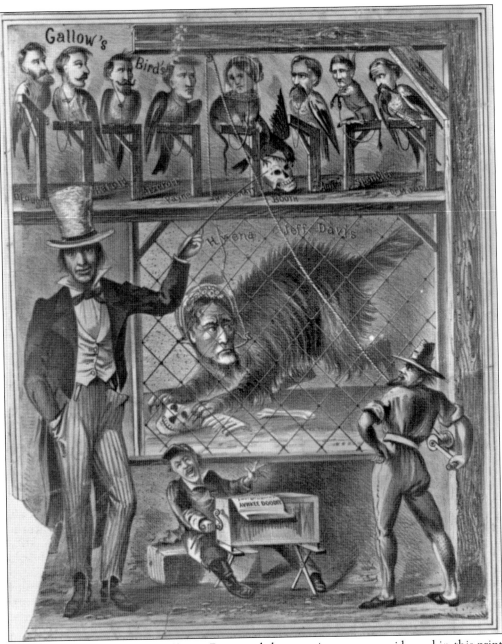

Hatred and hostility towards Jefferson Davis and the conspirators were evidenced in this print from shortly after the assassination of President Lincoln. Jefferson Davis is depicted as a hyena while the Lincoln conspirators are portrayed as "Gallow's Bird's," with their heads in nooses. Pictured from left to right are Michael O'Laughlin, David Herold, George Atzerodt, Lewis Payne, Mary Surratt, Samuel Arnold, Edman Spangler, and Dr. Samuel Mudd. John Wilkes Booth is shown as a death skull. (LOC.)

Eight

FAMOUS CIVIL WAR–ERA MARYLANDERS

Maryland was home to many prominent citizens during the Civil War, some loyal to the North and others loyal to the South. Marylanders Clara Barton, Frederick Douglass, and Harriet Tubman were well known outside of the state, while others, like Anna Ella Carroll and James Ryder Randall, were not household names but were just as important in the activities of the period. Even though Maryland did not secede from the Union, Maryland military men like Ralphael Semmes, Harry Gilmor, and Arnold Elzey would join the Southern cause and serve proudly in the Confederate States of America, while Henry M. Judah would serve proudly in the Union and attain the rank of brigadier general.

Thomas Swann, born in Alexandria, Virginia, was elected mayor of Baltimore in 1856. In 1864, he ran for governor of Maryland and won by just 9,000 votes. He took the oath of office on January 11, 1865, but would not assume the office until January 11, 1866. He was against slavery in Maryland and made it a key point of his inaugural address. He would later serve in the US Congress for 10 years. Swann died July 24, 1883, and is buried at Green Mount Cemetery in Baltimore, Maryland. (NARA.)

Anna Ella Carroll was the oldest of eight children of former Maryland governor Thomas King Carroll. When Abraham Lincoln was elected as president, she released her slaves and took an active role in pro-Union activities. During the war, she was involved in intelligence gathering for the Union and worked with Lincoln on issues with emancipation. (MSA.)

James Ryder Randall was born on January 1, 1839, in Baltimore, Maryland. He is the author of the poem "Maryland, My Maryland," which became the war hymn of the Confederacy during the war. He wrote the poem after hearing of the death of his dear friend Francis X. Ward, who was one of the 12 citizens killed during the Baltimore Riot of April 19, 1861. (MHS.)

Clara Barton was born in North Oxford, Massachusetts, and died in Glen Echo, Maryland. Her father was instrumental in her helping soldiers during the war, saying it was her Christian duty. She volunteered to serve as a nurse on the front lines of the Army of the James and became known as the "Angel of the Battlefield." After the war, she operated the Office of Missing Soldiers in Washington, DC. She is most famous for forming the American Red Cross in 1881. (LOC.)

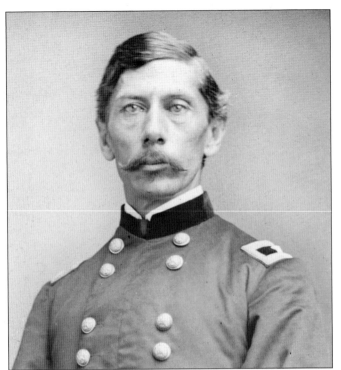

Union brigadier general Henry M. Judah was born June 12, 1821, in Snow Hill, Maryland. He was a classmate of Gen. Ulysses S. Grant at the US Military Academy. During the Civil War, he served mostly in Ohio, where he would be remembered for his 1863 role in helping to thwart Morgan's Raid, an incursion into Indiana and Ohio by Confederate cavalry. Judah died February 14, 1866, and was buried at Kings Highway Cemetery in Connecticut. (LOC.)

Confederate colonel Harry Gilmor was born at Glen Ellen estate in Baltimore County, Maryland, on January 24, 1838. He served as a member of Ridgely's Baltimore Horse Guards at the start of the war and was arrested and imprisoned in Fort McHenry after the military occupation of Baltimore in April 1861. He is best remembered for his raids near Magnolia Station in Harford County, Maryland, which would later garner his compatriots the name "Gilmor's Raiders." (LOC.)

The Honorable Charles Calvert was born on August 23, 1808, near Riverdale, Maryland. He founded the Maryland Agricultural College, the predecessor of today's University of Maryland, at College Park. During the Civil War, he served in the 37th US Congress from March 1861 until March 1863. He died on May 12, 1864, at the age of 55, and is buried in Riverdale, Maryland. (LOC.)

Maj. Gen. Arnold Elzey was born in Somerset County, Maryland, on December 18, 1816. He served in the US military before the war and later joined the Confederate cause and fought with the newly formed Confederate 1st Maryland Infantry at the First Battle of Manassas. After the war, he returned to Maryland and lived in Anne Arundel County until his death on February 21, 1871. (LOC.)

Frederick Douglass was born in Talbot County, Maryland, in February 1818. He escaped from slavery and was later recognized as an American social reformer, orator, writer, and statesman. Before the Civil War, he fought for the rights of both blacks and women. In 1863, he met with Pres. Abraham Lincoln to discuss the treatment of black soldiers. He died on February 20, 1895, after attending a meeting of the National Council of Women in Washington, DC. (LOC.)

Harriet Tubman was born in Dorchester County, Maryland, in 1820. She was an abolitionist and historian who escaped from slavery in 1849 and would later be recognized for her work in creating the Underground Railroad, which freed more than 300 slaves. During the Civil War, she worked as a cook, a nurse, and later a spy for the Union. She died on March 10, 1913, at the age of 93 in Auburn, New York. (LOC.)

Christian Fleetwood received the Congressional Medal of Honor for his service during the Civil War. Born in Baltimore, Maryland, on July 21, 1840, Fleetwood enlisted into Company G of the 4th Regiment United States Colored Infantry in August 1863. His Medal of Honor is now at the Smithsonian's National Museum of American History in Washington, DC. He passed away on September 28, 1914, at age 74 and is buried in Harmony Cemetery in Washington, DC. (LOC.)

Raphael Semmes served in the US Navy from 1826 to 1861. After the start of the Civil War, he served with the Confederate States Navy until 1865 and was the captain of the famous commerce raider CSS *Alabama*. Born in Charles County, Maryland, on September 27, 1809, Semmes would serve on the *Alabama* from 1862 through 1864, when it was sunk by the USS *Kearsarge*. He spent his final years in Mobile, Alabama, where he died on August 30, 1877, at the age of 67. (LOC.)

DISCOVER THOUSANDS OF LOCAL HISTORY BOOKS
FEATURING MILLIONS OF VINTAGE IMAGES

Arcadia Publishing, the leading local history publisher in the United States, is committed to making history accessible and meaningful through publishing books that celebrate and preserve the heritage of America's people and places.

Find more books like this at
www.arcadiapublishing.com

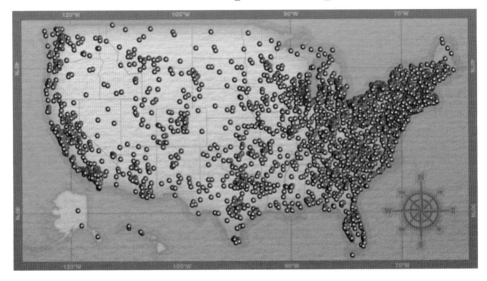

Search for your hometown history, your old stomping grounds, and even your favorite sports team.